HEADS HELD HIGH

Sam Warbuton, inspriational captain, who rose to the challenge
and became of the one of the players of the tournament

HEADS HELD HIGH

Wales' Rugby World Cup 2011

Foreword
Phil Bennett

Afterword
Max Boyce

Photographs
gettyimages®

SEREN

Seren is the book imprint of
Poetry Wales Press Ltd
Nolton Street, Bridgend, Wales

Explore 30 years of good books at
www.serenbooks.com

Foreword © Phil Bennett, 2011
Afterword © Max Boyce, 2011

ISBN 978-1-85411-571-3

A CIP record for this title is available from
the British Library

The publisher works with the financial assistance
of the Welsh Books Council

Printed by Akcent Media

Contents

Foreword

WALES failed by a whisker to reach the final of the 2011 Rugby World Cup but that should not obscure one stunning success. For the first time since the 2008 Grand Slam, the Welsh nation was in the grip of fevered excitement. People dared to dream.

Of course, the eventual reality was the narrowest of semi-final defeats to France instead of that yearned for final against New Zealand. But that should not detract from the significance of that wonderful week between the quarter-final victory over Ireland and that cruel night in Auckland.

For seven days the people of Wales believed. There was pride and deep satisfaction in being a Welsh rugby supporter and three million felt their emotions stirred.

Through playing some magnificent, exhilarating rugby – and conducting themselves so well – a young group of players captured the imagination of the public back home. There was a re-connection between the Welsh team and Welsh fans, something that was long overdue. Evidence of that was clear when 60,000 people turned up to watch the semi-final on giant screens inside the Millennium Stadium in Cardiff. It's impossible to imagine any other nation on earth where so many would turn up to see a team who weren't even at home.

It ended in tears, of course, with 14 courageous players denied, 9-8, following the decision to send off their young captain, Sam Warburton, for a dangerous tackle.

Cold-hearted realists will point out that Wales lost that game, then lost the third-place play-off, 21-18 to Australia. They will also point to a third defeat – a 17-16 reverse to South Africa in the pool stages – and condemn any sense of jubilation. They will be right. In professional sport defeats should always be regarded as a second-best outcome and no country has yet won a World Cup by settling for second best. But a young squad lost three games against top opposition by a combined total of five points and played such thrilling rugby along the way that I am genuinely excited about the future for this team.

Like most worthwhile achievements it began with sound preparation. A hard-headed coach, Warren Gatland, had his players together for three months before the tournament and used that time wisely. He twice took the squad to Poland for tough, exhausting conditioning camps that involved the now infamous cryogenic "deep freeze" chambers where players are turned into blocks of ice.

Some of those players have admitted they were close to cracking on those trips. They were put under such physical and emotional stress they didn't know if they were going to cope. It reminded me of going to South Africa with the Lions in 1974. Training at high altitude was incredibly tough for players who were totally unused to it. At first, there were some who felt they couldn't hack it – who complained their lungs were bursting – but the support of their mates pulled them through. That appears to be what happened with this current Wales squad and the result is a spirit of togetherness that people outside can never really understand.

Wales should have beaten South Africa in that first pool stage match, but somehow threw victory away. There followed a win over Samoa that was highly impressive. Not only were the Samoans one of the most improved teams in the world, but they had also been our nemesis in previous tournaments.

After that 17-10 victory, there was a crucial decision by Gatland to give other squad players their opportunity against Nambia. Morale was raised and so was the pressure on the first choice players with an 81-7 victory. Another bogey team of the past, Fiji, were hammered 66-0 and Wales were on to a quarter-final against familiar foes in Ireland.

It was after Wales had brushed aside an Irish team that had won every game – scoring three tries in a 22-10 victory – that I began to believe Wales were good enough to go all the way.

It didn't happen. A defiant defensive performance from the French, aided by that controversial sending off, meant Wales came up one point short, just as the French would in the final against the All Blacks. It was not all about fateful decisions, though. Wales missed too many goal-kicks that night and I could not have been the only person to see the irony in coach Neil Jenkins running on to the field with the kicking tee.

But there are three thoughts in my mind that already have me excited about the next World Cup in 2015.

The first is that youngsters such as Leigh Halfpenny, George North, Jonathan Davies, Scott Williams, Rhys Priestland, Toby Faletau, Dan Lydiate and Warburton are going to get better and better.

The second is that Gatland and his coaching team have shown they can lift the performance levels of the likes of Huw Bennett, Luke Charteris, Jamie Roberts and Mike Phillips – stretching their potential..

Thirdly, those wonderful Welsh supporters – whether the games be in Cardiff or across the border – will be there in full force... and full voice, too.

Phil Bennett
November 2011

SOUTH AFRICA 17:16 WALES

Tries: F. Steyn, Hougaard
Cons: M. Steyn 2
Pen: M. Steyn

Try: Faletau
Con: Hook
Pens: Hook 3

Frans Steyn	James Hook
JP Pietersen	George North
Jaque Fourie	Jonathan Davies
Jean de Villiers	Jamie Roberts
Bryan Habana	Shane Williams
Morné Steyn	Rhys Priestland
Fourie du Preez	Mike Phillips
Pierre Spies	Toby Faletau
Schalk Burger	Sam Warburton
Heinrich Brüssow	Dan Lydiate
Victor Matfield	Alun Wyn Jones
Danie Rossouw	Luke Charteris
Jannie du Plessis	Adam Jones
John Smit	Huw Bennett
Tendai Mtawarira	Paul James
Replacements	Replacements
Bismarck du Plessis	Lloyd Burns
Gurthrö Steenkam	Ryan Bevington
CJ van der Linde	Bradley Davies
Johann Muller	Andy Powell
Willem Alberts	Tavis Knoyle
Francois Hougaard	Scott Williams
Butch James	Leigh Halfpenny

Venue: Wellington Regional Stadium, Wellington   Referee: Wayne Barnes (England)

The worst possible start for Wales: Francois Steyn and Jacque Fourie celebrate South Africa's first try, after just three minutes

And Shane Williams is upended by Fourie

Wales face a green wall of attackers as Butch James looks to run

Wales respond in kind as Rhys Priestland looks beyond Jamie Roberts

Jonathan Davies offloads in the tackle

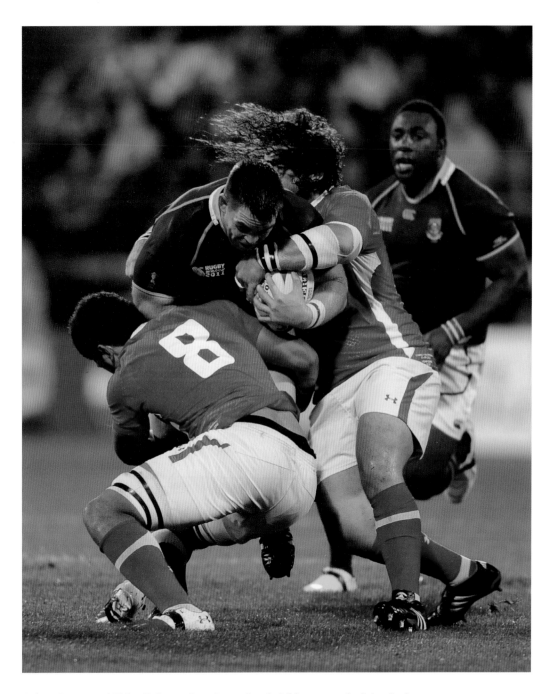

Adam Jones and Toby Faletau slow down South African captain John Smit

The tackle count mounts: Phillips on opposite number Faurie du Preez...

... and again on Morne Steyn

More tackles: Warburton drives on Schalke Burger...

... and Jonathan Davies combines with Huw Bennett to stop Jean de Villiers

In the second half Wales exert more pressure. Alun Wyn Jones takes a line out against Johan Muller...

... and Phillips is hauled back by Pierre Spies

Pressure is rewarded as Faletau charges past Morne Steyn...

... and under Frans Steyn for a deserved Welsh try

Wales celebrate. After so much pressure the momentum now seems to be theirs.

Captain Sam Warburton is held by a posse of South Africa tacklers

Warburton can scarcely believe it as Francois Hougaard steps through the Wales defence...

... to score South Africa's second try

At the final whistle Wales are left to rue a missed drop goal and penalty, and to ponder on the Hook penalty kick that never was. The game

had been within their grasp and the disappointment is tangible for players and (over page) fans alike

Wales 17:10 SAMOA

Tries: Williams
Pens: Hook 2, Priestland 2

Try: Perenise
Con: Williams
Pens: Williams

James Hook	Paul Williams
George North	Sallosi Tagicakibau
Jonathan Davies	George Pisi
Jamie Roberts	Sellala Mapusua
Shane Williams	Alesana Tuilagi
Rhys Priestland	Tasesa Lavea
Mike Phillips	Kahn Fotuall'l
Paul James	Sakaria Taulafo
Huw Bennett	Mahonri Schwalger
Adam Jones	Anthony Perenise
Luke Charteris	Daniel Leo
Alun-Wyn Jones	Kane Thompson
Dan Lydiate	Oflsa Treviranus
Sam Warburton	Maurie Fa'asavalu
Toby Faletau	George Stowers

Replacements	Replacements
Lloyd Burns	Ti'l Paulo
Gethin Jenkins	Census Johnston
Bradley Davies	Joe Tekori
Andy Powell	Manala Salavea
Tavis Knoyle	Jeremy Sua
Scott Williams	Eliota Fulmaono Sapolu
Leigh Halfpenny	James Soolalo

Venue: Waikato Stadium, Hamilton

Referee: Alain Rolland

A must-win game for both sides, Wales knew what to expect: big, bruising runs from forwards and backs alike. Their final tackle count was

142, in an uncompromising clash. Here the influential Paul Williams is held up twice

The tackles flew in from Samoa too. Priestland, who Samoa targetted in attack, gets the pass away but is about to receive attention from open

side flanker Maurie Fa'asavalu, who also high tackles him

Prop Anthony Perenise is just short of the Wales tryline line despite being driven forward by a team mate

This time Perenise makes it over, even with two Welsh tacklers on hand.

Two penalties from James Hook keep Wales in touch at half time

As the second half progresses Wales come more into the game. Here, Jamie Roberts does some damage through the middle

Warburton, having another outstanding game, presents the ball

After a couple of stumbles in the move Shane Williams finally takes Wales into the sunlight with yet another try

Job done. The stats will show Samoa on top in possession and territory and having spent almost three times longer in the Wales 22 than Wales did in theirs, but Paul James, Bradley Davies and Sam Warburton can applaud the Welsh support and look forward to the knock-out stages

Wales 81:7 NAMIBIA

Tries:	Scott Williams 3, Brew, Faletau, Jenkins, North 2 Davies, Lloyd Williams Byrne, AW Jones	Try: Koll
Cons:	Jones 6, Priestland 3	Con: Kotze
Pens:	Jones	

Lee Byrne	Chrysander Botha
Leigh Halfpenny	Danie Van Wyk
Jonathan Davies	Piet Van Zyl
Scott Williams	Darryl de la Harpe
Aled Brew	Danie Dames
Stephen Jones	Theuns Kotze
Tavis Knoyle	Eugene Jantjies
Gethin Jenkins	Johnnie Redelinghuys
Lloyd Burns	Hugo Horn
Craig Mitchell	Jané du Toit
Bradley Davies	Hainz Koll
Alun Wyn Jones	Nico Esterhuyse
Ryan Jones	Tinus du Plessis
Sam Warburton	Jacques Burger
Toby Faletau	Jacques Nieuwenhuis
Replacements	Replacements
Ken Owens	Bertus O'Callaghan
Ryan Bevington	Raoul Larson
Luke Charteris	Wacca Kazombiaze
Andy Powell	Rohan Kitsoff
Lloyd Williams	Ryan de la Harpe
Rhys Priestland	TC Losper
George North	David Philander

Venue: Stadium Taranaki, New Plymouth   Referee: Steve Walsh

It was a great day for centre Scott Williams, who scored Wales' only hat trick of the tournament (above and top opposite)

Lloyd Williams (above, bottom) also scored, part of a changed team which gave much of the squad its first game

Also on the scoresheet were Aled Brew and Alun Wyn Jones (opposite)

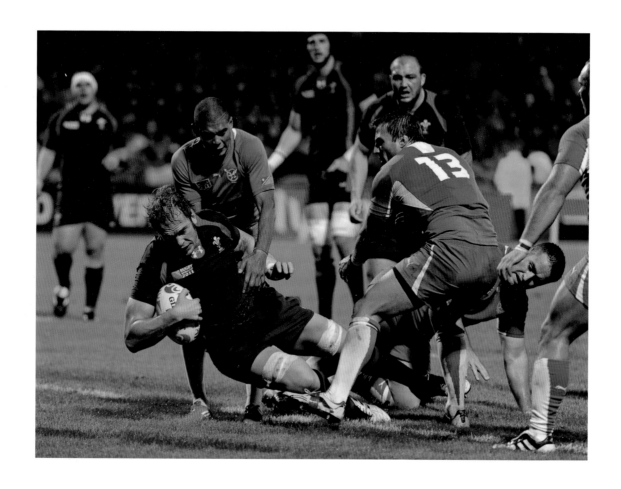

Gethin Jenkins made a welcome return, here bursting through the defence on his way to a touchdown

Lee Byrne was also influential, breaking the gain line, making tries and scoring Wales' eleventh of twelve

The backs scored nine of the tries but the forwards were dominant. Namibia found the scrum in particular a handful and had a prop yellow carded

Wales 66:0 Fiji

Tries: Roberts 2 Scott Williams,
          North, Warburton
          Charteris, Lloyd Williams
          Halfpenny, Davies
Cons: Priestland 5, Jones 4
Pen: Priestland

Lee Byrne	Iliesa Lomani Rakuka Keresoni
Leigh Halfpenny	Albert James Vulivuli
Scott Williams	Ravai Susau Fatiaki
Jamie Roberts	Gaby Lovobalavu
George North	Michael Tagicakibau
Rhys Priestland	Nicky Little
Mike Phillips	Vitori Tomu Buatava
Gethin Jenkins	Waisea Nailago
Huw Bennett	Sunia Koto
Adam Jones	Setefano Somoca
Bradley Davies	Leone Nakarawa
Luke Charteris	Wame Lewaravu
Ryan Jones	Rupeni Nasiga
Sam Warburton	Sakiusa Matadigo
Toby Faletau	Netani Edward Talei
Replacements	Replacements
Lloyd Burns	Viliame Veikoso
Paul James	Campese Ma'afu
Alun Wyn Jones	Mala Ravulo
Andy Powell	Akapusi Qera
Lloyd Williams	Nemia Kenatale
Stephen Jones	Seremaia Bai
Jonathan Davies	Vereniki Goneva

Venue: Waikato Stadium, Hamilton   Referee: Wayne Barnes

Wales' final group game was against another Polynesian team of big hitters and beguiling runners, but Jamie Roberts broke the defence for an early and settling try. And George North was soon operating in a similar vein (opposite)

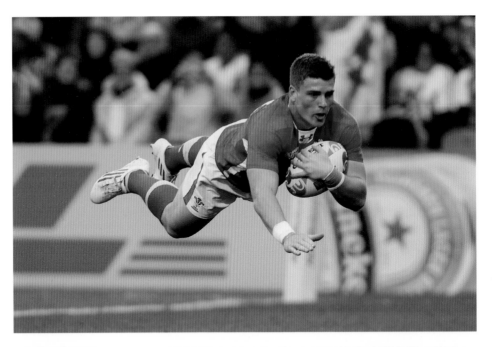

Tries flew in, with Scott Williams, Roberts again, Leigh Halfpenny and George North among the scorers

The Fijians resisted – fly-half Nicky Little stops Leigh Halfpenny with a crushing embrace

Lee Byrne forces a turnover from Ravau Susau Fatiaki

Charteris rises into the wet night sky for a catch as comfortable as the Wales victory

Ireland 10 : 22 Wales

Try: Earls	Tries: Williams, Phillips, Davies
Con: O'Gara	Cons: Priestland 2
Pen: O'Gara	Pen: Halfpenny

Rob Kearney	Leigh Halfpenny
Tommy Bowe	George North
Brian O'Driscoll	Jonathan Davies
Gordon D'Arcy	Jamie Roberts
Keith Earls	Shane Williams
Ronan O'Gara	Rhys Priestland
Conor Murray	Mike Phillips
Cian Healy	Gethin Jenkins
Rory Best	Huw Bennett
Mike Ross	Adam Jones
Donncha O'Callaghan	Luke Charteris
Paul O'Connell	Alun Wyn Jones
Stephen Ferris	Dan Lidiate
Sean O'Brien	Sam Warburton
Jamie Heaslip	Toby Faletau
Replacements	Replacements
Sean Cronin	Lloyd Burns
Tom Court	Paul James
Donncha Ryan	Bradley Davies
Denis Leamy	Ryan Jones
Eoin Reddan	Lloyd Williams
Jonathan Sexton	James Hook
Andrew Trimble	Scott Williams

Venue: Wellington Regional Stadium, Wellington   Referee: Craig Joubert

Wales, clearly up for the game

Mike Phillips makes a relieving kick from an early ruck

Best possible start: Shane Williams dives under Keith Earls' tackle to touch down... and celebrate (opposite)

Shane Williams busy in defence: a high kick is taken (opposite) and Sean O'Brien is bravely held up over the Wales line

Brian O'Driscoll, Ireland's talismanic captain, is stopped in his tracks by Huw Bennett...

... and goes flying as Ireland try to get back on terms

Flanker Stephen Ferris hurdles a couple of Welsh tacklers (above) but is less fortunate as Warburton and team mates carry him backwards (opposite)

Adam Jones covers across as O'Gara kicks tactically

In another game of big hits three Welsh tacklers combine to halt Paul O'Connell

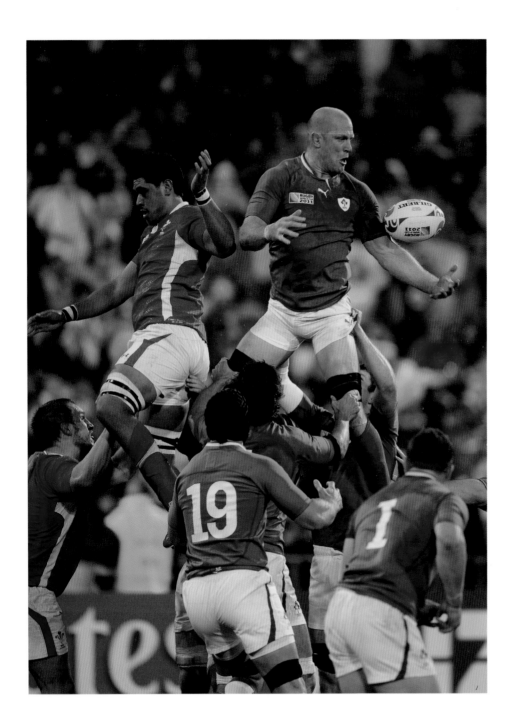

O'Connell steals a line-out (opposite), and Rob Kearney stretches the Welsh defence with a strong run

Alun Wyn Jones can only look on as Keith Earls takes Mike Phillips over with him. The tv match official gives the try and with O'Gara's conversion the score is 10-10

Wales respond in kind a few minutes later, as Phillips beats Tommy Bowe to the corner. Referee Craig Joubert consults the tv match official again but there's not much doubt about his verdict. 15-10 to Wales

The technique looks sound and Rhys Priestland was unlucky to hit the post with two penalties

Priestland relieves Irish pressure with a kick from hand

The pressure continues. Leigh Halfpenny beats Rob Kearney to the high ball (opposite) and Mike Phillips defends the ball in a double Irish tackle

Jonathan Davies hands off prop Cian Healy...

... and crosses the Irish line for Wales' third and decisive try

After more staunch defence, the final whistle and Wales are in the semi-final

Jubilation. Belief is high after a tough match against a good Irish side

Skipper Warburton and coach Gatland shake hands knowing that Wales have every chance now

Wales 8 : 9 France

Try: Phillips   Pens: Parra 3
Pen: Hook

Wales	France
Leigh Halfpenny	Maxime Médard
George North	Vincent Clerc
Jonathan Davies	Aurélian Rougerie
Jamie Roberts	Maxime Mermoz
Shane Williams	Alexis Palisson
James Hook	Morgan Parra
Mike Phillips	Dmitri Yachvili
Gethin Jenkins	Jean-Baptiste Poux
Huw Bennett	William Servat
Adam Jones	Nicolas Mas
Luke Charteris	Pascal Pape
Alun Wyn Jones	Lionel Mallet
Dan Lidiate	Thierry Dusautoir
Sam Warburton	Julien Bonnaire
Toby Faletau	Imanol Harinordoquy
Replacements	Replacements
Lloyd Burns	Dimitri Szarzewski
Paul James	Fabien Barcella
Bradley Davies	Julien Pierre
Ryan Jones	Fulgence Ouedraogo
Lloyd Williams	Francois Trinh-Duc
Stephen Jones	Jean Marc Doussain
Scott Williams	Cédric Heymans

Venue: Eden Park, Auckland   Referee: Alain Rolland

Welsh fans at Eden Park get in the mood

James Hook gives them something to cheer about with a 7th minute penalty

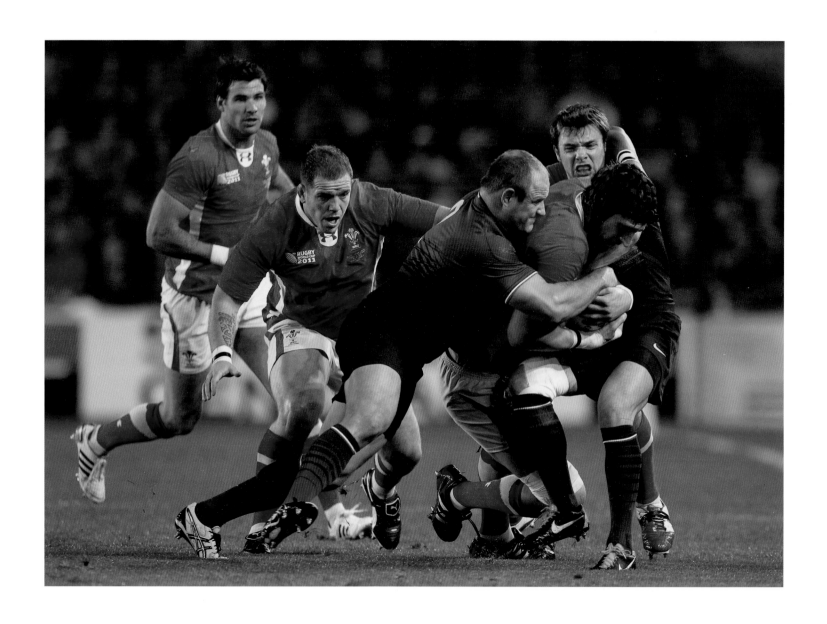

Luke Charteris can't find a way through William Sevat and a fellow French tackler (above), and Jamie Roberts sets off on a charge, one of many during the night

Opposite: A setback for Wales as Adam Jones is forced off after ten minutes with a calf injury. Paul James replaces him.
Above: George North tries to shake off a French tackle

Two angles of the tackle that changed the match, and with it Wales' World Cup

It looked bad and the French players are already concerned and protesting as Clerc hits the turf

The half-hearted scuffle following the tackle suggests the players know the likely outcome

Referee Allain Rolland brandishes the red card and Wales are down to 14 players with 60 minutes to go

Not the end to his World Cup that he would have wanted: a distraught Warburton watches the game from the touchline

Gatland ponders his next move, while Long and Howley study the game. Is this the moment he considered *all* his options?

In the meantime Wales battle on with spirit: the stalwart Alun Wyn Jones takes a line-out

George North gathers under pressure from Morgan Parra (opposite) and Jamie Roberts makes another run upfield

James Hook attempts a drop goal to get Wales back on terms

Mike Phillips starts from a ruck, spots a gap and goes...

Huw Bennett and Alun Wyn Jones see the possibilities...

... and Phillips grounds for the try which gave Wales hope

... and something to celebrate, in New Zealand...

... and in the Millennium Stadium. Wales 8 France 9

Wales turn up the pressure with runs at the French defence by Toby Faletau and the rest of the team

Alun Wyn Jones and Imanol Harinordoquy both get hands on a throw (opposite) and Shane Williams weighs up his options

Mike Phillips tries to set the Welsh backs going

Toby Faletau finds himself surrounded

A long distance penalty to Wales after a ruck infringement. Leigh Halfpenny makes good contact

Halfpenny jumps for a better view and kicking coach Neil Jenkins looks on anxiously. The kick just clips the underside of the bar.

The minutes count down. Wales go through over twenty phases as the clock turns red and they try to manoeuvre Stephen Jones into good drop-goal range. Here, the tireless Jamie Roberts is stopped by four defenders

France may have forgotten how to attack but they defend in numbers against Toby Faletau

The final whistle. Joy for France, now World Cup finalists, but despair for the exhausted Wales, a man down for an hour

The France players celebrate but Shane Williams lets out a roar of disappointment that his World Cup career won't end in a final

The Wales team regroups before leaving the field

Wales walk off, applauding their supporters

And back home in Wales, emotionally exhuausted supporters ponder how close they had been to the World Cup final

Wales 18 : 21 Australia

Tries: Williams, Halfpenny   Tries: Barnes, McCalman
Con: Jones   Con: O'Connor
Pens: Hook, Jones   Pens: O'Connor 2
                                     Drop Goal: Barnes

Wales	Australia
Leigh Halfpenny	Kurtley Beale
George North	James O'Connor
Jonathan Davies	Adam Ashley-Cooper
Jamie Roberts	Berrick Barnes
Shane Williams	Digby Ioane
James Hook	Quade Cooper
Mike Phillips	Will Genia
Gethin Jenkins	James Slipper
Huw Bennett	Tatafu Polota-Nau
Paul James	Salesi Ma'afu
Luke Charteris	James Horvill
Bradley Davies	Nathan Sharpe
Dan Lidiate	Scott Higginbotham
Toby Faletau	David Pocock
Ryan Jones	Ben McCalman

Replacements	Replacements
Lloyd Burns	Sala Faingaa
Ryan Bevington	Ben Alexander
Alun Wyn Jones	Rob Simmons
Andy Powell	Radike Samo
Lloyd Williams	Luke Burgess
Stephen Jones	Anthony Faingaa
Scott Williams	Robert Horne

Venue: Eden Park, Auckland   Referee: Wayne Barnes

The fans are ready, the dragon substituted

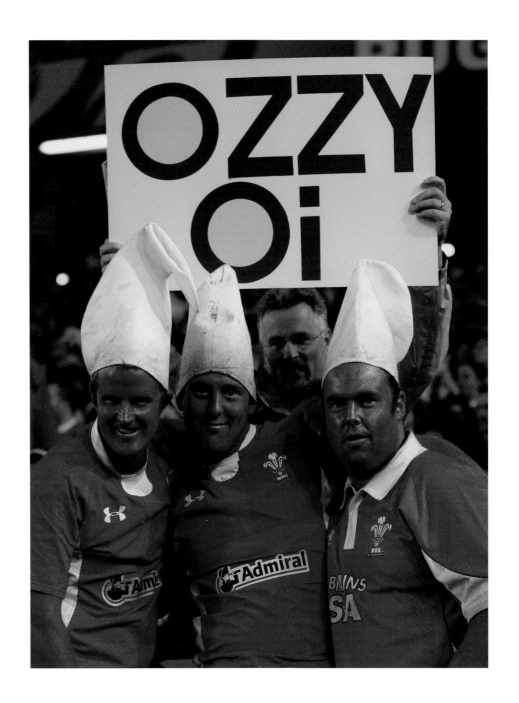

The always competitive Australians hijack the red smurf photo opportunity

The Welsh verdict is clear...

... but Sam Warburton can only watch

The final anthem for Wales in the World Cup

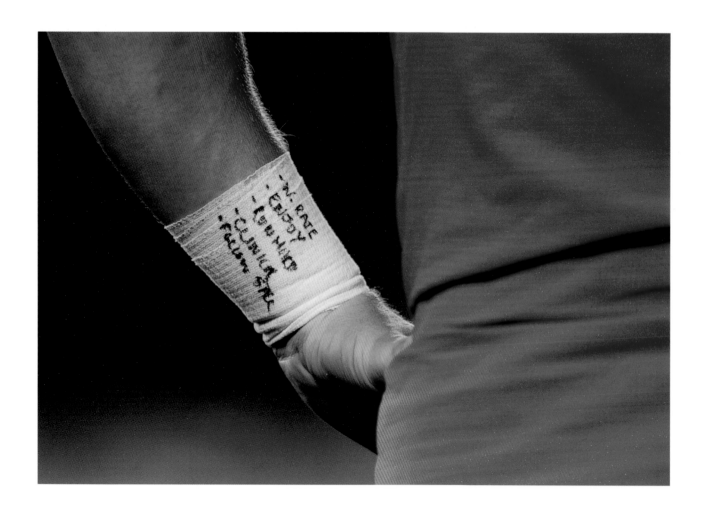

George North has his instructions to hand

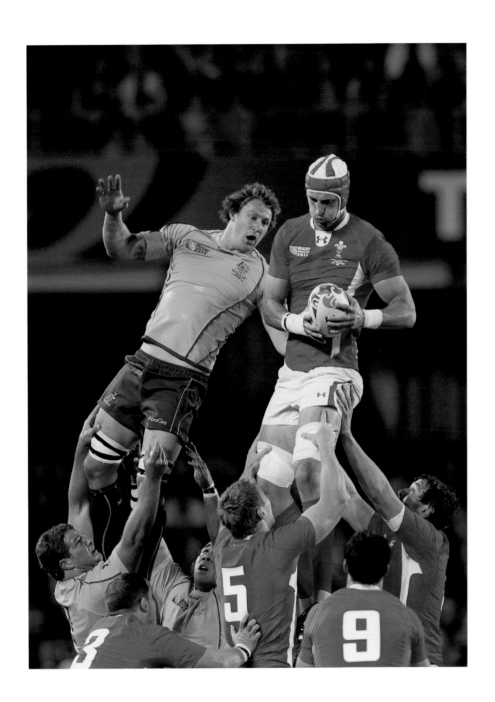

Luke Charteris secures the Wales line-out

Jamie Roberts tests another defence

Swift hands and it's all too easy for Berrick Barnes to slip through the Welsh defence for a try

Wales compete: Ryan Jones and Nathan Sharpe tussle in the line-out

Toby Faletau puts in yet another big tackle as Australia press

Both sets of forwards strive for the upper hand

Jamie Roberts on the move again, faced by Adam Ashley-Cooper

Scrum half Will Genia gets the better of Roberts in the tackle

Early in the second half Shane Williams goes over for a final World Cup try, and Huw Bennett celebrates. 10-8 to Australia: Can Wales pull off a comeback?

A ferociously contested maul, with Australia's David Pocock at its centre

Bradley Davies is tackled on the charge

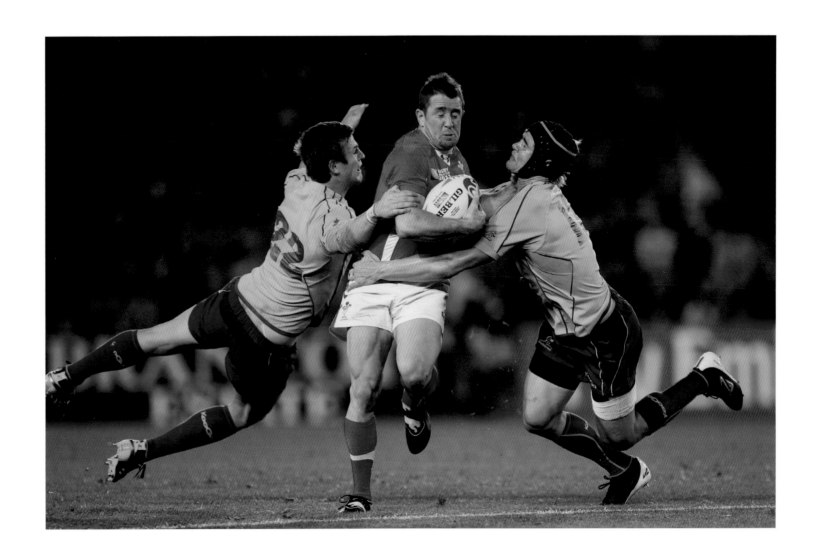

Shane Williams is sandwiched by Australian defenders...

... while Ryan Jones offloads, balletically

Australia had already stretched to 13-8 when Berrick Barnes, who had moved to fly half on Quade Cooper's injury, kicked a drop goal

Barnes' opposite number, Stephen Jones, tries to get an attack going as Australian cover moves across

Wales press forward. A bloodied George North is hauled back

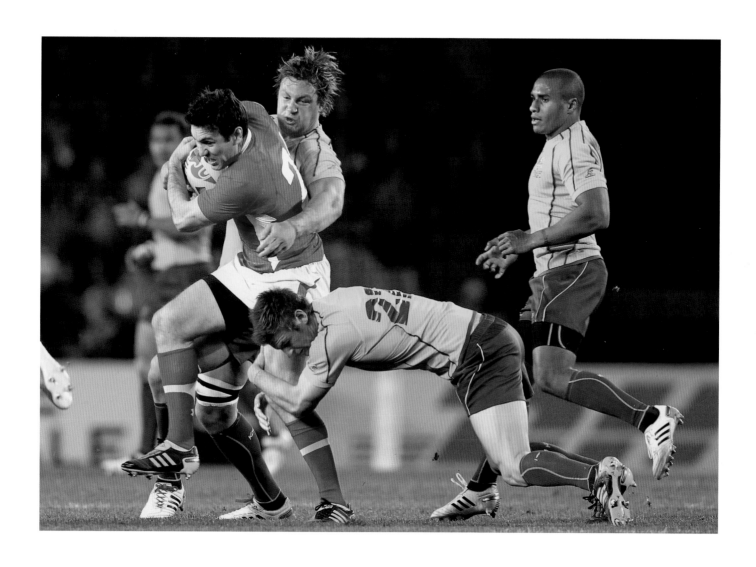

Stephen Jones battles forward with two Australian tacklers in tow

Australian number 8 McCalman scores unchallenged from five metres out

Australia celebrate their second try. With 15 minutes to go they scent a win

Sean Edwards and Warren Gatland can only look on as time slips away

Welsh defenders drive back Radike Samu

Wales turn again to their big ball carriers. Andy Powell punches through a ruck...

... and finds a winger to run past in Digby Ioane

Australia in control at the line-out on their throw

Leigh Halfpenny steps inside the defender to score in injury time.

The final whistle, and Wales must settle for fourth place

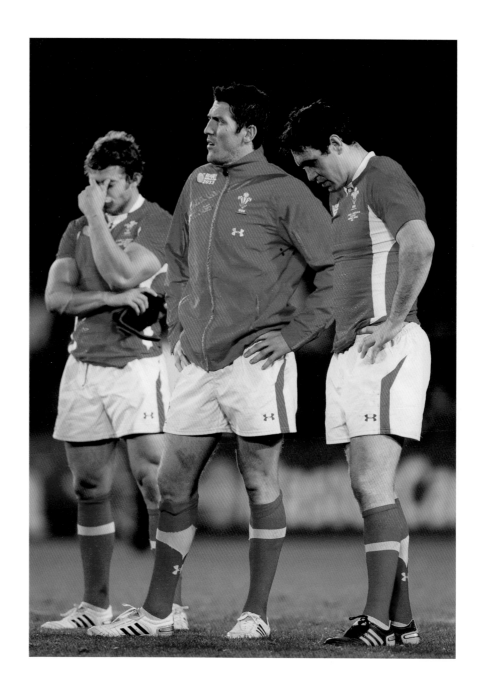

Despite this defeat there is still a sense of achievement for a young Wales side, with the future before them. They leave the field with heads held high

The Backroom

Warren Gatland, Coach

Sean Edwards, Warren Gatland and Rhys Long, Head of Performance Analysis, in discussion

Neil Jenkins, Kicking Coach

Robert Howley, Assistant Coach

Robin McBryde, Forwards Coach

Sean Edwards, Defence Coach

Mark Davies, Physiotherapist

Roger Lewis, WRU Chief Executive,
with Gerald Davies

Afterword – The Unforgiving Moment

The World Cup in the Land of the Long White Cloud turned out much as many people had predicted with the All Blacks, the host nation, narrowly beating France in the final by a single point. New Zealand's long wait was over at last, but not without much drama and incident.

All through the night (Ar hyd y nôs)

New Zealand had this great disaster,
    All through the night,
Carter's leg was put in plaster,
    All through the night,
Long the nation has lamented,
But now at last they sleep contented,
The Long Black Cloud at last relented,
    All through the night

But no-one had predicted that Wales would be the country that was to make the greatest impression in the tournament.

From the very first game against South Africa in the pool of death and in every subsequent game they were a breath of fresh air, capturing the hearts and minds of the people of Wales and beyond. They were suitably humble in victory and gracious in defeat. There was only unreserved praise and unswerving support for this young side who played with honesty and courage and with no little flair and skill.

At Number 10 our flag was flying,
    All through the night,
Downing Street were edifying,
    All through the night,
When Cameron rose to share the glory,
Of Wales' still unfolding story,
I even thought of voting Tory,
    All through the night

They ran with the freshness of youth and with a smile that had been missing from Welsh rugby.

In pro-sport the margins between success and failure are so small and so difficult to measure. Those often cruel margins are so thin as to appear to have only one side.

And so it was in the semi-final against 'Les Bleus'... Sometimes, something that seems meant for you just passes you by. The Fates are against you. The Fates... the apportioners of destiny and fortune, whom the Gods fear. Clotho who spins the thread, Lachesis who measures the thread and Atropos who cuts it.... The decision that went against us in the semi-final was the unkindest cut of all.

My mobile phone kept on tweeting,
    All through the night,
Gatland even thought of cheating,
    All through the night,
That tackle wasn't meditated,
Rolland's call is still debated,
I was heavily sedated,
    All through the night

The fact that nearly 70,000 people flocked to the Millennium Stadium that fateful morning, sleep still in their eyes, all to watch the game on a big screen, was testimony to the intoxicating fever that had gripped the nation like never before. The price of admission to the ground... *was the colour red*. Red was the colour that opened the doors and the clicking turnstiles, Red was the colour that allowed you access to all areas... Red was the colour of the backstage pass,

They came from Crymych and Caernarfon, Blackwood, Pyle and Aberavon, from the four green fields of Wales. They sang with painted faces all beneath a piece of slag. Their flags unfurled, their colours pinned to the mast, carrying their songs like a like a soldier carries his rifle to war... Only for their hopes and dreams to be undone in one *unforgiving moment*. A moment that broke the heart of the nation. The crowd at the stadium, their voices stilled, watched with horror and disbelief at the events unfolding on the other side of the world. Their dream was about to end. Their time in the sun was over. Their disappointment was real and heartbreaking as they emptied into the still waking streets of Cardiff.

Much has been written about Cryotherapy. The scientific study of players' recovery and the tortuous training regime the Welsh team were subjected to in the raw freezing chambers of Spala in Poland. This arctic experience prepared them well for the brutal intensity of the early games against South Africa and Samoa. Their recovery and fitness conditioning was testimony to that intense preparation.

But what of the supporters, the forgotten faithful followers...? They had no such preparation to help them recover from the devastation of the defeat against France.

Great cryogenic chambers will have to be built able to hold thousands of Welsh supporters in their icy depths, to aid their recovery. Only then can we march on England in 2015 properly prepared.

By then Team England will have recovered from the controversy and shame that followed them in New Zealand.

The English team were disappointing,
    All through the night,
The R.F.U were reappointing,
    All through the night,
Tindall's head was clearly showing,
Above the dwarves his team were throwing,
The board's review is still on-going,
    All through the night

Everyone will have their views on the unfortunate sending off of young Sam Warburton, but everyone will be unanimous in praising Wales' young talisman as a player of rare ability and a person of the highest integrity with a previously unblemished disciplinary record. A warrior whose demeanour and willingness to face the inquisition that followed is testimony to his honesty and bravery.

In one frame of film the World Cup was wounded and Wales' remarkable journey had come to an end. To Welsh followers, and I suspect many others, this was the defining moment of the World Cup in 2011 and one they will always remember. When all the bunting in the streets of Auckland has blown away, when the weld on the open top buses has cooled and the dwarves have gone back to Snow White's cottage, they will remember what might have been in that one unforgiving moment.

Sometimes, though only rarely, more can be achieved in defeat than victory and though there were no selfish gains or ribboned coats, this young Welsh side earned the respect of the rugby playing world and in so doing re-established Wales as a creditable force in world rugby and on a world stage. That is no mean achievement and something for which they and their management should be proud and a nation grateful.

There is no denying that New Zealand deserved to win the World Cup after all those years in the wilderness and though *Black* was the colour of the ribbons tied to the Webb Ellis Cup in Auckland 2011... *Red* was the colour of admission.

Max Boyce
November 2011